ANIMALS in DANGER

Blue Whale

Rod Theodorou

Heinemann Library
Chicago, Illinois

Designed by Ron Kamen
Illustrations by Dewi Morris/Robert Sydenham
Originated by Ambassador Litho
Printed in Hong Kong/China

05 04
10 9 8 7 6 5 4 3

Library of Congress Cataloging-in-Publication Data
Theodorou, Rod.
        Blue whale / Rod Theodorou.
                p. cm. – (Animals in danger)
        Includes bibliographical references (p.) and index.
        Summary: Explains the habitat and behavior of the blue whale, why it is endangered,
and how children can help save whales.
        ISBN 1-57572-263-1 (lib. bdg.)   ISBN 1-58810-443-5 (pbk. bdg.)
        1. Blue whale—Juvenile literature. 2. Endangered species—Juvenile literature. [1. Blue
whale. 2. Whales. 3. Endangered species.] I. Title.

QL737.C424 T52 2000
599.5'248—dc21
                                                                            00-025763

Acknowledgments
The author and publishers are grateful to the following for permission to reproduce copyright material:
Ardea London, p. 6, Ardea London/ Francois Goltier, p. 5; BBC Natural History Unit/ Doc White, pp.
12, 13, 17, BBC Natural History Unit/ Jeff Foott, p.16; FLPA/ Fritz Polking, p. 4; Greenpeace/
Cunningham p. 27; Heather Angel, p. 25; Mike Johnson, pp. 7, 8, 9, 14, 15, 18, 19; NHPA/ David E .
Myers p. 26; Oxford Scientific Films/ Daniel J. Cox, p. 4, Oxford Scientific Films/ Mark Cawardine, p.
23; Still Pictures, p.21, Still Pictures/ Michel Gunther, p. 4, Still Pictures/ Roland Seitre, pp. 20, 22, Still
Pictures/ Paul Glendell, p. 24.

Cover photograph reproduced with permission of Phillip Colla Photography.

Special thanks to Henning Dräger for his comments in the preparation of this book.

Every effort has been made to contact copyright holders of any material reproduced in this book. Any
omissions will be rectified in subsequent printings if notice is given to the publisher.

Some words are shown in bold, **like this.** You can find out what they mean by looking in the glossary.

Contents

Animals in Danger

manatee

mountain gorilla

giant panda

All over the world, more than 10,000 animal **species** are in danger. Some are in danger because their homes are being destroyed. Many are in danger because people hunt them.

This book is about blue whales and why they are **endangered**. Unless people learn to **protect** them, blue whales will become **extinct**. We will only be able to find out about them from books like this.

What IS a Whale?

Whales are huge swimming **mammals.** They spend all their lives in the ocean. They have to come to the **surface** to breathe air.

There are 83 different **species** of whale. The largest is the blue whale. The blue whale is also the largest animal that has ever lived!

What Do Blue Whales Look Like?

Blue whales have a very long thick body with a huge head. They have a long flipper at each side, a small fin on the back, and a huge tail. They are blue-gray in color.

Blue whales can grow as long as a six-story building is high. They weigh the same amount as 30 elephants, or 4,000 eleven-year-old children!

Where Do Blue Whales Live?

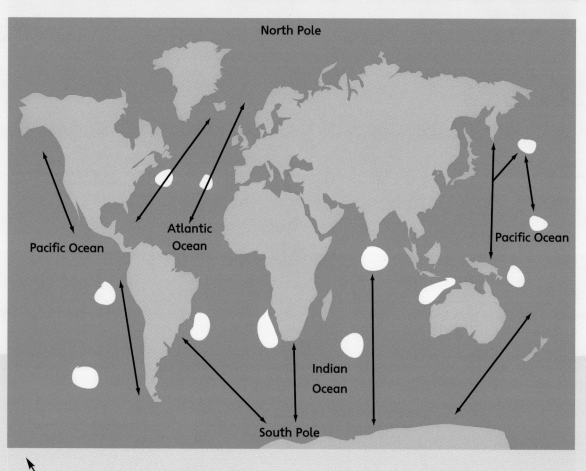

North Pole

Pacific Ocean

Atlantic
Ocean

Pacific Ocean

Indian
Ocean

South Pole

↕ migration routes ⬠ winter mating areas

Blue whales swim all over the world's oceans.
Some blue whales stay in one area. But most
migrate huge distances every year.

Every spring, migrating blue whales swim toward the **North Pole** or the **South Pole**. They eat lots of food there. They return to warmer waters in the fall, and stay there for the winter.

What Do Blue Whales Eat?

The huge blue whale eats tiny food! It eats tiny shrimps called **krill**. The whale opens up its mouth like a giant scoop and lets in huge amounts of water and krill.

The whale pushes the water through its **baleen** plates. These are like long **bristles** in its top jaw. The krill, and other tiny creatures and small fish, stick on the plates and are eaten by the whale.

Blue Whale Babies

Blue whales live in family groups of about two or three, called pods. The mother whale usually has just one baby, which is as long as a two-story house is tall.

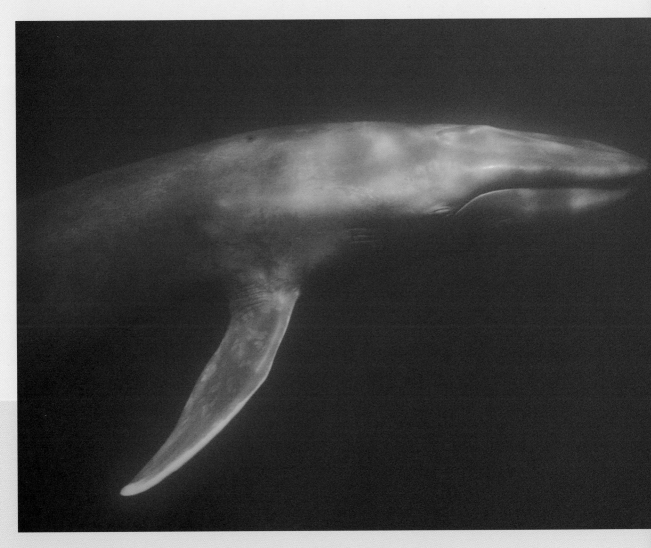

The baby is called a calf. The calf feeds on its mother's milk for about eight months. It grows very quickly, gaining as many pounds every day as a grown man weighs. Soon it is huge!

Caring for the Calf

Adult blue whales are so big they do not have many enemies. Sometimes killer whales, called orcas, may threaten a young blue whale calf. The whales in the picture are orcas.

If the whales are in danger they can swim away very fast. They can also dive down very deep and hold their breath for up to 30 minutes.

Unusual Blue Whale Facts

Blue whales are incredibly big. The amount of **krill** that an adult whale eats every day weighs more than a semi truck. Even its tongue weighs more than a full-grown elephant!

All whales **communicate** with each other using "whale song." The blue whale's songs sound like a deep rumbling noise. Their sound travels under the water for a very long distance.

How Many Blue Whales Are There?

One hundred years ago there were about 335,000 blue whales alive. Then people started to hunt and kill more and more whales. Now there may be fewer than 4,000 left.

By 1960 the blue whale was almost **extinct**.
Between 1860 and 1960, about 350,000 blue
whales had been killed by whaling ships.

Why Is the Blue Whale in Danger?

Over 100 years ago people started to build large ships to hunt whales. The whalers sailed all over the world, killing whales with a large spear called a harpoon.

The dead whales were then cut into pieces. In some countries, people still hunt and kill whales. The whale's **blubber** is melted to make a kind of oil. Whale meat is also used for food.

The blue whale is also in danger from **pollution**. Chemicals dumped into the sea are eaten by **krill** and other tiny creatures. When the whales eat the krill they can become sick.

Noise made by ships' engines and oil drills also harms the whales. The noise is so loud the whales cannot hear each other's songs. This may mean they cannot find other whales to **mate** with.

How Is the Blue Whale Being Helped?

In 1946, many countries decided to stop the killing of certain whales. They formed the International Whaling Commission (IWC). The IWC has **banned** all whaling now.

Conservation groups like Greenpeace and the World Wildlife Fund (WWF) are also working to save the whale. They are trying to stop countries that ignore the IWC and still kill many whales.

Blue Whale Fact File

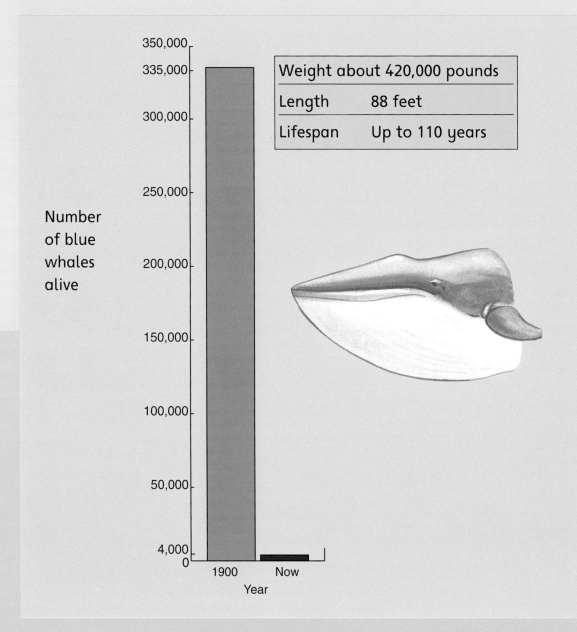

Number of blue whales alive (y-axis)

350,000
335,000
300,000
250,000
200,000
150,000
100,000
50,000
4,000
0

1900   Now

Year

Weight	about 420,000 pounds
Length	88 feet
Lifespan	Up to 110 years

World Danger Table

	Number that may have been alive 100 years ago	Number that may be alive today
Giant panda	65,000	650
Bengal tiger	100,000	4,500
Black rhino	1,000,000	2,000
Mountain gorilla	85,000	500
Florida manatee	75,000	2,000

There are thousands of other animals in the world that are in danger of becoming **extinct**. This table shows some of these animals.

How Can You Help the Blue Whale?

If you and your friends raise money for the blue whales, you can send it to these organizations. They take the money and use it to pay conservation workers, and to buy food and tools to help save the blue whale.

Greenpeace
14306 U Street N.W.
Washington, DC 20009

Ocean Alliance and Whale Conservation Institute
191 Weston Rd.
Lincoln, MA 01773

World Wildlife Fund
1250 Twenty-fourth Street N.W.
Washington, DC 2007-7180

More Books to Read

McDonald, Mary A. *Blue Whales*. Chanhassen, Minn.: The Child's World Inc., 1998.

National Wildlife Federation Staff. *Endangered Species: Wild & Rare*. Broomall, Penn.: Chelsea House Publishers, 1999. An older reader can help you with this book.

Robinson, Claire. *Whale*. Chicago, Ill.: Heinemann Library, 1999.

Glossary

adult	grown-up
baleen	type of bone that whales grow in their jaws
banned	not allowed
blubber	thick layer of fat some animals have just beneath their skin that keeps them warm
bristle	thick hair
communicate	talk or make yourself understood
conservation	looking after things, especially if they are in danger
endangered	group of animals that is dying out, so there are few left
extinct	group of animals that has completely died out and can never live again
krill	tiny shrimp-like animals that live in the sea in huge numbers
mate	when a male animal and a female animal come together to make baby animals
migrate	when animals travel long distances to a better place to find food or a more comfortable place to live
North Pole	northernmost part of the earth
oil	thick liquid that can burn easily
pollution	trash or noise that spoils a place and can hurt animals
South Pole	southernmost part of the earth
species	group of living things that are very similar
surface	top of the water

Index